B   O

D0732940

B O R D E R S

Mary Crow (signature)

POEMS BY MARY CROW

FOREWORD BY DAVID IGNATOW

BOA EDITIONS, LTD. ▪ BROCKPORT, NEW YORK ▪ 1989

ISBN: 0-918526-70-1 Cloth
ISBN: 0-918526-71-X Paper

LC #: 88-63975
First Edition

Some of these poems, or earlier versions of them, originally appeared in the following magazines: *American Poetry Review, Ploughshares, New Letters, Beloit Poetry Journal, Massachusetts Review, Southern Poetry Review, Kansas Quarterly, Mid-American Review, Quilt, Wooster Review, Negative Capability, The Green Mountains Review, Hampden-Sydney Poetry Review, Abraxas, Foreign Exchange, Pulp, Alembic, Four Zoas,* and *Aspen Anthology.*

"Talcahuano: Souvenirs" won the James Wright Prize for Poetry from *Mid-American Review.*

"Not Volcanoes, Not Minerals," "Montserrate," "The Heat in Madellin," and "My Barrow Stones" first appeared in *Woman Poet—The West,* ed. Carolyn Kizer (Woman Poet, Inc., 1980).

"Going Home" was reprinted in *Quilt* (Fall, 1981).

"Idle Afternoon" was reprinted in *Three Rivers Poetry Journal*'s special "Discoveries" double issue, 1981.

"Going Home" was included in the chapbook, *Going Home* (Lynx House, 1979).

"Idle Afternoon," "Girl Floating on Air," "Not Volcanoes, Not Minerals," and "Going Home" were included in the chapbook, *The Business of Literature* (Four Zoas, 1981).

"Foreign Streets" was reprinted in *Anthology of Magazine Verse and Yearbook of American Poetry for 1979,* ed. Alan F. Pater (Monitor, 1980).

"After a Certain Number of Years, the Light Changes" was reprinted in the anthology, *Plaza of Encounters* (Latitudes Press, 1981).

Publications by BOA Editions, Ltd., a not-for-profit corporation under section 501(c)(3) of the United States Internal Revenue Service Code, are made possible in part with the assistance of grants from the Literature Program of the New York State Council on the Arts and the Literature Program of the National Endowment for the Arts, a Federal Agency, as well as grants from private foundations, corporations and individuals.

Cover image: "Yellow Crosses IV," Quilt by Nancy Crow
Cover Design: Daphne Poulin
Typesetting: Visual Studies Workshop, Rochester, NY
Manufacturing: McNaughton & Gunn, Inc., Ann Arbor, MI
BOA Logo: Mirko

BOA Editions, Ltd.
A. Poulin Jr., President
92 Park Avenue
Brockport, NY 14420

To the memory of my mother,
Rachel Kensett Crow,
and my father,
Glenn Frank Crow

TABLE OF CONTENTS

FOREWORD

Mary Crow's poems are their own best inducement. I am simply here, I believe, to point out that these poems are the culmination of years of thought and feeling, with which we are identified. They are the witness to her life, a life not any more complex than our own, except that she is Mary Crow, and we read her for the person she is, which, for us all, is the main attribute of living.

Whatever led her to spend a year in South America, traveling, researching the poetry of South American women, is not a question that needs an answer. It is simply a way of stating Mary Crow's difference from us, and yet her resemblance to us in her eagerness to find herself through others. Traveling is one means many of us take in such an undertaking, and so along the path of her research she is struck and deeply shaken by the ordinary people of these South American countries who live out their lives on the edge of starvation in hallucinatory states of hope, faith, love, and sex. She becomes involved. She writes to illuminate and perhaps free herself of her involvement through the exercise of compassion in her poems. For compassion sets one apart from the victim at the same time that one has learned to experience the victim as oneself—a tricky business, but a necessary one for self rescue, and it brings with it the guilt of such knowledge. After all, she is there to find herself, also in the hallucinatory states of hope, faith, love, and sex of others.

Burdened with self-seeking, the poems nevertheless glow with colors of place and time, are clamorous with prayerful voices and reek with the naked smells of prayers. An ancient Indian world assails her. Its stones, dust, and bones nearly overwhelm her, as do the faces and bearing of these suffering souls. And so, travel and research that were meant for her to arrive at some harbor of rest and self realization only return her to these United States. Here she sees, though in different forms and conditions, what she has lived through in the Southern Hemisphere, and it gives birth to poems of renewed social and private anguish, in her own country. The reader begins to realize in retrospect that the circumstances written about her

South American trip are like some huge metaphor to prepare us and herself for what was to happen to her here. Though the book ends on a note of hopeful love, it is not without a certain air of reservation which permits the self a way out: how a house is built with an escape exit in case of fire.

The poetry of Mary Crow is as we would expect of an artist deeply troubled by her experiences. The writing is taut, lean with the struggle to persevere and become its own true cause; and by the grace and power of her art, the poems in *Borders* are kept from vanishing into the pain itself, thereby making a voice and presence for herself that is the fulfillment of her search for self. In short, she is the quintessential artist who is made whole by the very processes of art. Let us welcome Mary Crow to the company of poets.

—David Ignatow

BORDERS

I

FOREIGN STREETS

I am walking as fast as I can,
shifting my shoulders to slide past
men or the knives of thieves.
And, yes, I need a man,
a man to protect me
from those hot looks on the street
which are hate or lust,
or both. Yes, yes,
I want him to go with me
into the restaurants,
into the streets.
Yes, I admit it:
living alone is dangerous
and I am weary of fear,
weary of clutching
my dusty belongings
under my arms.
Maybe I'm weak,
but I'm going to repeat it:
I want a man.
I'm sick of thinking about myself,
of closing my heart
against the day's dozens
of cripples and amputees,
the blind man with festering sores,
the filthy kids who sleep on the streets.
And my anger,
yes that especially:
everyone tells me
everyone is a thief.
Tonight all the corners are filled
with soldiers with their first beards
and machine guns.
I want to slink past.
You won't like my saying it,
but I dream of men

breaking down the glass walls
to get at me,
and the police don't come.
There is so much water.
I wake up crying,
"My child, my child."

FESTIVAL

The dancers group in the plaza:
costumes of silver armor,
eyes of their masks bulging,
their horns, teeth,
red, green, yellow.
Heads covered with wigs
of yarn, legs cased
in baggy red and yellow pants,
they stamp
the monotone of drums.
And the furry bear
follows the octopus,
both already a little drunk;
with his stuffed tentacles
the octopus beats on the bus
as it tries to nudge
the dancers out of its way.

The Quechuas
have twenty names
for degrees of drunkenness
and in the hot afternoon
we have used them up.
Dancers have come from every village
on Lake Titicaca
for this contest,
and they keep on
dancing, weaving patterns
in their hot plastic gear,
swaying and stumbling.
Bottles of beer and pisco
line the curbs,
and shards of empty bottles glitter.
Here and there a dancer lies
slumped against a building
sleeping it off,

his face in vomit.
In the aisle of the jammed bus,
a drunk dances
all the way home.

TRAVELLING ALONE

I.

Gila monsters whip into the underbrush
leaves tremble under my feet
and the sun bathes me
in its heavy heat   I drag
the deep constellations of affections
sky dull blue and empty
pinpoints of pain in my chest
toward the burning beach
There is nothing to fasten to
I contain the edges of space

II.

New city   I stand looking at the gulf
green and flat below   Houseboats like arks
rock beside the highway
Today I've lost the melody
stretched between horizons of darkness
Even this unbelievable garden
of green leather leaves
of orange   pink   red blossoms
is mere bougainvillaea   palms
and pomegranate trees
danger of colors

III.

The net bloomed in the lake
on that lazy day   blue haze
on the blurred hills   green rice stalks
shimmered beside the boat
as we bailed and laughed
We fried the tiny fish   then ate them

sprinkled with lime juice and salt
washed them down with beer and cane alcohol
That night when I read you poems of travel
the room was full of echoes
as we lay down together

IV.

While I waited   they killed
the suckling pig   and I could hear it
screaming   They gutted it   scraped it
It hangs now fat and sleek
from a tree in the garden   where I accept
the bitter tea handed to me every morning
the first mouthful on trust
the cup promising home

GRAVEYARD

Chancay, Peru

Up and over sandhills,
the grave robbers lead us
toward the ancient graveyard
they plunder by night,
landscape a monotonous grey
undulating under a misted sky.
Flakes of stone at our feet
flush green and violet.
From a hill, we look down toward
endless grave pits;
the sun comes out,
grey gentles toward tan.
Bones lie on the slope
where we descend,
and we can see skulls blazing,
some clouded
with tags of flesh, hair.

Shards everywhere—
white and red mostly,
molded with toad handles.
We walk around
grave timbers,
some still lining pits
where the mourners of Chancay
braced them
four hundred years ago.

Under this sun, hot now,
we cross the field of tombs,
climb hills toward other tombs
until we stand
high above them all,
look back toward
our own beginning

across skulls, leg bones,
and the presence is not death
or grief.

It is time
I feel sit down beside me.
I look toward the sea,
blue beyond green fields,
beyond the tan sand
littered with bleached bones,
striped shrouds, red shards.

We open the picnic
and drink our beer,
still a little cool
under the blazing southern sun,
then eat our sandwiches,
our local olives.
At last we run
downhill toward the sea,
running for the love of it,
to feel our bodies
working hard, our laughs
whipped out of us,
and tattered.

TALCAHUANO: SOUVENIRS

I stand on the dock
in the dying light
that sets horizon, boat bow
and wing on fire,
watching the dump trucks
fill up with silver fish.
Peddlers ply
smoked fish, clams,
bundles of rubbery seaweed.

And the color of the sea
is changing from dark green
to celadon:
dusk slides down its crests
as I take pictures
I know cannot transmit this light,
my heart's buoyancy.
A man pauses, posing,
and I raise my camera.
"No," he says, "just joking!"
"Please," I answer,
"Then I will have
a Man of Chile."
He is struck, stops,
flings out his arms
and puts on a smile.
I take him.

Chile flows inside me—
the little bird carved from coal,
the clam digger's net-like basket—
recuerdos.
The secret craftswomen
coil pigs and pitchers of clay,
drying them in sunlight,
firing them in backyard holes
with gathered dung.

And I have memories
of people who offered me
KAF, the closest thing to coffee,
homemade bread and honey
on my travels.
Along the road I picked blackberries,
reaching high to find
the ones less dusty.

Sitting under arbors
I laughed with wives
until their shy husbands showed up
bringing a burlap bag
of mussels from the sea
or leading a golden colt they called "El Rey."

And then the mass
in a private home near Purema
where I knelt on the filthy floor
before the long table
laid with a white cloth, candles, flowers,
wafers and wine.

La vida dura—
I can't say
the people pray for nothing more.
But the grey green sea
breaking over grey rocks
and green cliffs rising beside it,
patient oxen pulling their carts,
girls on horseback at dusk
after a long day of work—
these things can be reckoned up
and re-counted
when they wake
on a winter night.

THE PYRAMID AT CUERNAVACA

Temple within a temple, double temple,
honeycomb of lava,
rock of lace
with the broken features of a man,
I sit in your shade
thinking of a man
entering the dark temple of a woman.
My lava and earth
resist. I cling to your hands,
I mold them.
I ask you to hold me
in a certain way. I let you move me
and I move with your hands, but the shape
we are making is mine.
Honeycomb in the stone, cinder
of lace, burnt out rock
flung from the moon.
The plaza of the dead rises
into my mind,
covered with weeds.
Skulls line the shelves
and my fingers pull themselves
to your smoothness, the bone
cupping the skin, leather.
A woman has entered the plaza
and kneels at her lover's feet in the weeds
as I watch from the shadow
at the top of the temple
in the hot afternoon.
Beside me, the face in the stone
changes; I trace
my fingers over the rough edges.
Faces of the serpent, blunt-nosed
and worn, look toward the city.
Tiny black-eyed daisies push up
from stone. Rock of lace,

black fingers of hair
above a cut profile,
sockets shadowed in the dark room,
honeycomb of light,
your warm skin.

NOT VOLCANOES, NOT MINERALS

I am being followed.
Actually, I'm hardly aware
of the faint footsteps behind me.
Laughing too loud,
I don't hear
the scurrying of animals.
I can't see the light in the car
parked beside the forest
as I lie down in the dark.
Bundles of twigs for my bed,
I look up at the horned moon.
A moth with fabulous markings,
gold and black,
I rise out of the darkness
on a path of moonlight.
Fish flutter in the deep water
behind my eyelids
waking me out of myself,
and I see a man
watching me, writing down
what I am.

BORDERS

II

WEIGHT OF THE DAY

Glare, hot lights, relentless
groan of traffic, legless beggar
whose monotonous voice
pursues me down the street:
Señorita, por favor, señorita…
At breast level, two machine guns:
black eyes, deep and empty.
Everything is so clean!
No droppings, only a chirping
from the top of a tree.
From a distant street,
the dry plucking of a siren
trills our taut nerves.

SAFETY IN WAR

He picks up a stone
and examines it:
What was its use?
What was the shape
of their cooking pots?
How did they tell time?
This is a red stone,
painted or blood-stained...

A priest guided the tribe
to this fertile valley
where they built their city,
charted the chronology of kings,
here a woman fermented juice
and got them drunk.
Goddess eight feet tall
with her head of twin snakes,
necklace of human hands,
hearts, a skull,
and her hands are claws.

In the same field,
beans, squash, pumpkins, corn;
after the weeding,
the making of grass mats,
sandals, canoes, weapons.
The rack of skulls:
the ritual ball game
in front of it.

Life exists for the sake
of newness.
Archeology of suspense.
The patina of loneliness
is polished;
contradictory data

are catalogued
with the minutiae
of rain, dust, and bones.

The diet of rain gods
is human hearts,
still steaming,
red flowers
on the stem
of the offering arm.
And music:
sticks rasped
over notched bone.

The sun drains
the earth of color;
this is a dry country.
But here there are 22 stages
for drunkenness,
and war, and captives
to sacrifice.

In his own country
another man
is picking up a stone.
How can he use it?
And why is it red?

GIRL FLOATING ON AIR

Lying on her back, hands raised
Above her head, she lies flat
On the bed of wire.

She seems to sleep, becalmed
In the moment's weather, waiting
For someone.

Now they are braiding
Something between her fingers,
Between her toes,

And wetting her stretched-out body —
Is it to purify? —
As she shivers there.

Her eyes are closed; no color
Hooks us in. This is the thing
As it is,

And (imagining a better
World) we wait with her
For the cattle prod.

A VIEW OF THE SEA

Twice a day it burns, at dawn and dusk,
the pelicans rise from their sand bar
in a flight so weighted down it is almost not flight
while I try to see the sand, the hills,

as if I had never seen them.
Standing alone on the beach
I face sea, white surf, grey rocks.
    (Skyscrapers touched by fire

        lose their daytime dirtiness;
        windows flame around the man who stands
        alone on the balcony, angling
        for a touch of breeze, some relief from fire.

        The dust that is filtering over his papers
        covers his office chair
        with a fine film
        as if the first handful of dirt
        had been thrown into his grave—

        all that is behind him at this hour.
        Better not to think about death,
        about where he is heading, whether to take
        the freedom he has. He looks down

        and his legs burn with the effort of standing.
        Eight hour days of make-work!
        A lifetime of nothing! But at least
        he gets paid, dresses well, has plenty

        to eat. All these rumors of corruption!
        He sighs, turns his back on the dark leap.)
On the shore, I look into the waters,
green where shallow, but darker further out,

the pull and tug, tug and pull,
churning under their white caps.

AMAZON

We crossed the watery boundaries
of countries, and in the old boat
sluggishly moved down the plain of water.
The toothless boys told us the story
of the fishes. There is one fish
that searches for the openings of the body,
burrows into the ass or vagina,
then sticks its fins out on both sides
and cannot be removed.
These fish eat you inside out.

The other fishes, red and grey,
rise to the surface, their huge backs
breaking the water, in the gleam
of sunset, and the boys shudder telling it.
Only the red ones are dangerous.
Humped and blazing in the afternoon's vermillion,
they put a spell on the young boys
and when a boy seizes a red fish
to make love to her, the fish
grabs his penis in her vagina,
carries him out into the river
and he is hers forever.

"That bitch!" one boy mutters
as a large fish surfaces,
then he remembers us and falls silent.
Both banks had been green forests
when the boat chugged up the plain of water
blue with its pictures of skies.
But now the water is rippled golden
and the sky, clouds, river,
red with fishes.

IDLE AFTERNOON

The wooden door swung open turns the entrance
into a sitting place, a savage throne,
with the door itself the high back;
and she can sit on the threshold.
Bold angles of sunlight and shadow
pattern the door's weathered wood.
Only the white porcelain doorknob
breaks the geometric lines
with its roundness, its curves.

The wind may pick up any minute now
and blow the woman's hair,
still out of place from the last gust.
Through thin cotton, she can feel
with back and thigh how much like stone
the wood's become—warm, steadfast, worn.

In the yard the box elder
that has spread into a gangly shape
rises still above its little puddle of shade.
There is nothing else to see from this perspective.
No path crosses the hot backyard
and no living thing ventures into the noonday sun.
Only the woman, her hands folded into her lap,
sits in the doorway and stares into space
looking out from her shelter of shade,
fixed in the death of the afternoon.

A CHANGE OF PLACE

Shrapnel of morning:
sword-like leaves of the house plant,

forks, knives, scissors.
Light shatters through the window

bags, cans of food, boots,
bits and pieces of makeup.

I am here, not here.
Grey cough of cars rises,

red tiles undulate
green hills undulate:

shimmer of garbage burning.
Counting out the minutes,

I am here, not here.
This year, next year, anytime.

Never. The machine
of my routine is broken.

I want to go home,
put it together again.

THE REAL THING

*"The real motive, the real thing attained is
the revelation of what you can perceive
beyond the fact."*
—Robert Henri, *The Art Spirit*

The fact is he is only the father.
The fact is he is arrested anyway,
dragged to prison and questioned
about his dirty, subversive son.
He tells them he knows nothing.

The fact is he knows nothing.
The fact is he is forced to kneel
in front of the shit-filled toilet.
Tell us where he is or in you go.
I know nothing, absolutely nothing.
Whatever you do, I'll still know nothing.
They duck his head in and hold him.

His body thrashes, his shoulders sag.
They pull him up. Where is he?
They yell. Tell us, where is he?
His lungs wheeze: I don't know.
The fact is they push his head in again.

This is only one incident among many,
only one incident in another country.
It is not happening to you, to me.
The fact is this father is only a father
in a poem, a construct of sound.

I HAVE MY INSTRUCTIONS

I have my instructions
I know what I should do
if you are killed
who should be called
at what number
what arrangements to make
before I slip out of the apartment
back to my old life
and try to pretend
that you never existed
In any case there was no future
and the freedom
I released you to every day
was your one true element
Now you will wholly belong
to freedom
There is the roar of engines
over the rooftops
as I look out
somehow expecting a knock
There is a tiny window in the door
that looks out
into the hall
but the hall is empty
You told me
you would show me
how to keep myself from death
but I wake up in the morning
and think it has arrived

MONTSERRATE

They climb the mountain on their knees
Dirty, their patched pants
breaking open
the dark-faced lady sobbing
A child holding his crutch over his head
hauls his body up a foot at a time
and the sky is so beautiful
full of green fingers of pine
below clean clouds
the blue color of church windows
At the top in the church
racks of tiny candles
50 pesos each
burn for the dead
for the living
In that dark church
the moreno Christ looks darker
blood streaming down his arm
down his leg
The people think he is theirs
but the priest has wrapped him
in plastic to protect Christ's knees
from their wet kisses and dirty fingertips
They have crawled up here
their bloody knees burning
and like Christ they wear drops of sweat
on their foreheads and backs
Here they are in this high church
in their temple of trees
the sough of wind a music
the white and blue of sky
church and Mary
a cleanness they desire
But Christ
the Christ of Sorrows
collapsed above the pulpit
leans on his arm

and can't raise his head
to look at them
They have left their crutches
their walking sticks
here for him
here for love
and think they will walk again
without their cross
Urchins pass through the pilgrims
as they arrive
looking for worshippers
blinded by tears
or tourists
snapping the worshippers
the urchins' faces hard
their eyes beady as Christ's

THE HEAT IN MEDELLIN

In Beiria Park
the armless and legless
look up from grey pallets
beside the church
with staring eyes.
Dirty children are rising
from their concrete beds
over the warm air vents
and the blind man
calls out his lottery numbers.
Morning in Medellin:
my heart is already hard.

Rubber stamps drum in the bank
and the eyes of waiting people are dull.
As I leave, a woman walks up,
stark naked; people laugh
and say she's crazy.
She walks into the reflecting pool,
her dimpled flesh quivering, oblivious,
and I envy her.
In Junin Street the kiosks display
pale freesias with their smell
of death; stiff yellow callas
for the grave are being watered
while the suburbs have no water
and the poor drink from the river.
Every morning we read about children
who died. And there is no light,
because the rains are late this year.
From their glass stands, vendors sell
peaches and grapes imported from Chile,
from California.
Further down the block,
a vendor makes the sign of the cross
over his cigarettes
as he begins his day.

Morning in Medellin:
a man sits down on the sidewalk
and lifts his trousers
so we can pity his open wound.
Morning in Medellin:
here comes the crazy man in his rags,
bearing his cardboard box
with the red chicken and the white,
one pink rose, a small flag, and a ribbon
displayed on top. He holds it all up
as he talks to God
from his perfect world.

ON THE BUS FROM TEMUCO

Pensamientos, a flower called thoughts;
happiness of the house,
alegria de la casa—
plain coleus and geranium;
my thoughts open into another language,
dark-leafed reverses,
white dust, black light,
a heat that withers.
Back in the public market
a woman opened a basket,
pushed aside damp hay:
pale green eggs from the country.
Flavor of the country, *sabor del campo,*
she says, the best!
Green pebbles in the dark sand
of a straw beach—
perfect, quotidian,
word I'm beginning to love:
el cotidiano.
And the water under the bridge
is almost the same opaque green,
milky and pale, on its broad pebble bed.
Filthy!, my mind says,
but my eyes say, Beautiful!
Children are digging at the edge
as the bus hunkers down
the pits and scars of this road.
My mind jumps like a fish
in the pale green air,
dusty now like a veil
behind which everything glimmers!
The days open into gardens,
glimpses of patios
cool in the distance,
and the endless sweeping of a broom
across brick and stone:

daily, basket of eggs beside the dusty hovel,
daily, grey green water to drink,
daily, bruised pears in the garden.

SHOPPING IN SANTIAGO

In the market, clams, still closed,
tan shells ribbed and grainy, the valve darker,
and the huge conger, not really eel,
its one eye congealing, skin a slimy grey,
pink shrimps in their husks
with the tiny sticks of their antennae stiff...
I point to what I want,
make do with words I have, and pay.
It is still difficult to learn
what I am being taught.
Flesh, meat, smell of shit;
in the parks, couples necking
and my own skin tingling and alive.
Out of the grave the archeologist took
the figure of a clay skeleton,
his gigantic penis erect up to his eyes;
then he dusted off a clay couple fucking,
the woman on her stomach,
head turned back toward her lover,
both pairs of eyes open and round,
fixed perhaps on death,
not veiled in surrender,
their lips turned downward
as if in sorrow.

I speak it aloud: I am middle-aged,
well preserved. On my trip south,
a 23-year-old wanted me to come with him
for a week of water skiing,
but I said to myself, He's seen
too many European movies. O smooth skin!
I was tempted to forget death;
but sex would only remind me:
the little deaths of ejaculations...
That's not enough to explain a whole museum
of erotic sculptures dug out of graves.

Or why the odor of decay sets the body
trembling. We pretend we don't like
sensitivity of the anus, smell of armpits.
After cooking, take out the garbage—
shrimp shells, fish bones and guts,
husks of peas. Spray everything
with fake pine so we can think virgin forests
and purity! Sex is gluttonous and pulls
the body closer to bones;
moving inside the self, inside the other,
it wants more and more. Inadequate words
for desire! Penis moving among guts,
membranes, juices. Gills of the vagina
opening, closing.

LETTER FROM CHILE

You say you are working hard, sometimes things go well,
sometimes ill. The metro takes you to your job,
so you read the censored paper as you go.
Leaning forward in the seat, you press your thumbs
into your tired eyes, black spots spreading across
the blank screens of your eyelids. And suddenly
you see your garden, small and ill-kempt but comforting,
its high walls covered with vines of red grapes.
You feel so tired you would like to stretch out
in spite of this mob of people, trains screeching.
You are so tired of waiting for trains, for destinations.
Sometimes you look around—you can't believe it—
things which seemed to be as bad as they could get
keep getting worse. So now you say, "Believe
the impossible, imagine that that man over there
is listening, will tell some colonel everything I say."
You marvel at how leaves unfold in your garden.
You are so exhausted and feel as if you were falling
down an endless tunnel; you fear that at any moment
your large body, aging and out of condition,
will hit the blank wall at the bottom.

ROSE RED

In the presence of thistles
don't tell me
about the stupid
red face of the rose.
　　　　—Jerzy Harasymowicz

But I need to have it on my table
for the calming scent, that rosy color
that lulls me as I sit here
chewing my toast, mulling the news.

Beauty can be stars on barbed wire,
red flare against the night
brave enough to make a flag of.
Or beauty: rosy glow from the skyline.

And if beauty, truth.
When the red-headed woman,
standing naked in a line of naked people,
flew at the soldier, scratched his face

with her red nails, she cut red lines
down his cheeks. When they
strapped her onto the stretcher,
shoved her feet first into flames,

her hair became fire.
What did beauty get her—
with her hair blazing as the rose,
her skin white as my tablecloth?

IN THE HOUSE OF FLOWERS

We were the serpent's people
tracing his sprung length
into stone,

beating goats
into their stalls
in the evening; barefoot

among cactus and anthills,
we had always come
to this place

to thank the sun,
carrying bundles
of casachica on our backs

up those stony paths to him.
Among tiny blue
and yellow

flowers, we
stopped high on the hill,
hailing the dawn's face of fire

on our distant lake.
Then we descended,
but part way,

and we came
into the old ball court,
that fatal game. Later,

we left the palace, dropped down
to our thatched huts, brats,
sugar cane,

mangy dogs
yapping at our heels
as we dreamed of athletes, stone

circles. The rules of the game.
We had our chores, too,
almost as

fatal—
hoeing corn under
the sun, chasing hawks

from carcasses, carrying
water for others' baths.
The babies' crying

was our star.
What did the sun care?
Broken columns, fallen walls,

stone tumbled on stone, wasp nests,
anthills, and the dust
of stones.

COMING HOME AFTER
A SPEECH ON REVOLUTION

We pass a tree among trees,
its limbs a convention of crows,
and we think sickness, death.
Final thoughts! Suicide notes!
Is everything beyond repair?

The sun twists and twists from that tree;
you say: I will bring the rivers back to you.
You do not have to pass from door to door,
polishing the blue figures of conjecture
like old metal, selling yourself.

This will be the ideal revolution:
Everyone will join this time.
All the doors will fly open
and victims love thieves.
Sons will follow their mothers into battle.

Dusk starts to sweep up scraps of words
as I try to hold onto *ideal!*
onto *everyone!*, onto *doors!*, onto *rivers!*
Crows fly up cawing and the hanged
sun is lowered from the tree.

AFTER A CERTAIN NUMBER OF YEARS,
THE LIGHT CHANGES

Abstraction growing bones,
landscape built up
grain by grain, sand
cut by the thin line
of a river, pelvis

and flower in the changing
light, and I am here.
All afternoon wind
around the house;
tips of the willow

yellow as summer
writhe before my window.
What was my first poem?
Myth of the Ghostly Lover?
A decorated landscape?

One thing I know:
I am rooted in the landscape.
In the year of the horse,
I am starting again.

How do I get back?
Under the current thought,
a thought, and under that,
bare bones, bare bones,
the light changes.

This is the dream world,
the earth of the body.
In the year of my poem,
the mote in the light
is a minute horse flying.

BORDERS

III

ON THE OTHER HAND

On the other hand, I love you.
The blossom loops over the gnarled roots
and fleshy leaves
canopy the bedroom window.
Rumble of tires, gears quarreling far away—
the bird squawks angrily in the garden.
Your arm flutters on the pillow.
I am learning to live
with the parasitic plants
and that marvelous vine
that lifts its phallic white rod at the door
out of a red heart.
Your heart beats
and I am getting used to it.
Even the orange bougainvillaea
no longer surprises,
or the hibiscus, yellow and red,
nudging the pink impatiens.
Heavy avocados bulge in pairs
from the little tree,
and the hairy ferns
climb the hill to my apartment.
Your shoulder shifts,
as you settle in,
and I know every muscle,
every curve
of the branching pepper plant
hung with its golden lanterns.

A MAN WHO LIVES ALONE IN ATHENS

Night after night,
he wakes in the dark
after sleeping five hours.
Who are you courting?
his friends laugh.

But he lies in bed
under the shadow of the acropolis
remembering the cold moonlight
years before when they came
in their black uniforms

to drag his father off to Dachau
and how his dying mother, years later,
refused to speak to him,
turned her back,
left him nothing.

He prefers to live alone.
I sleep better,
he tells his friends.
The single bed in the corner
has a wine-colored coverlet.

Beside it a small heater
is cold, the paint along
the baseboard mildews.
Soon the moon will come in,
a cold silence to add

to his silence. He opens
the gate, lets in a forest of stars.

MY BARROW STONES

I live on an island
and there I tend
a little heap of stones.
I keep busy
rearranging them.
Sometimes
I pile them up
to form
a rocky phallus
pointing skyward,
a cairn
marking the way
to nowhere.

Or I arrange them
in rings,
signs of eternity
or concord,
circles
circling each other,
embracing earth,
enclosing nothing.

I have wrung them
and gotten
sore hands:
They would not cry.
I have rubbed them:
They would not
catch fire.

Sometimes
I plant my stones
in the rocky soil,
make a sign
at the sun

and demand
that he make
my stones grow.

I dig them up.
After all,
I have
to live
on this island.

IN THE DEPTHS

Mother, I bit your face
and the blood ran down your neck
as I held you tight.
I could feel it, warm and sticky,
on my breast.
And the scene changed.
I saw my face in a mirror,
lines deepening
into a mask of wrinkles.
You were gone, Mother,
and I was a monster,
awkward and thick,
clawing the mirror.

In the depths of the glass
I could see a statue
in the form of a draped woman.
A trickle of water
fell from your hands
and became a spray,
became a stream
that carried me
away from the mirror
and into the woods.
The stream became a river
smoking in a cold dawn
toward a large city.
And I looked up
into the Gothic ceiling
of a cathedral.
Mother, Mother,
where are you?

HARD THINGS: COLORADO

Home: Goat mountain, frozen hillside,
shale rubble on the slope
where I struggled to climb
against the slipping and slippery
scrim up to the small caves,
lairs of mountain lions, or old graves
full of fine dark dust.

I used to drive home, feeling the weight
lift off my shoulders mile after mile.
Friends asked how I could bear
living so far out, but I loved
driving toward the light, turning into the gate,
the dog and horses racing to greet me,
the sound of the river pounding against
my ego, my pitiless self.

GOING HOME

The eye of the dead beer can lives in my headlights.
The Elkhorn Motel flashes "Vacancy"—
only a couple of truckers too tired for love
have registered.
Near the top of the hill,
a sign commands,
"Thru Traffic Take Center Lane,"
and I drive straight thru without slowing down.

The five women I've just left
are driving home in separate cars.
Late at night, after wine,
we have been talking
about how to meet a man,
about what to do with ourselves.
One woman says,
"I'm in love with my right hand,"
and we all laugh.

We park in front of dark houses
and enter to silence.
I turn on a light,
grab a cold beer from the fridge,
sit by myself in front of the TV.
The light registers in my eyes
but my mind is driving toward love.

Maybe I could post a sign
flashing at the end of my lane.
Maybe I could stand beside the road
and hitch a ride with a trucker.
Maybe I could drive up to a full motel
and knock at the first door.
Maybe I could get in the car and keep driving,
driving thru loneliness
to the other side.

WANDERING WITH BASHO

(After reading Basho's *The Narrow Road to the
Deep North and Other Travel Sketches*)

I follow the white crumbs of stars,
foraging words, revising the map's
narrow roads toward winter.

What I can discover covers
my hard bed of earth, my tea and bread—
daily beginning again.

Purify? Purify? I am trying.
Even my bones ache.
My wet sleeve, scythe made of moonlight.

A cow bell shatters the sharp air,
a rooster measures the dawn:
Light comes on slowly.

ABOUT THE AUTHOR

The winner of a Poetry Fellowship from the National Endowment for the Arts in 1984, Mary Crow has previously published two chapbooks of poems, *Going Home* (Lynx House Press, 1979) and *The Business of Literature* (Four Zoas, 1981). Her poems also have appeared in several anthologies, including *Poetry Ohio* and *Wingbone: Poetry from Colorado*, as well as in many literary magazines, including *American Poetry Review, New Letters, Prairie Schooner, Beloit Poetry Journal, North American Review,* and *Ploughshares.* In 1988 she read her poems in Yugoslavia on a Fulbright Creative Writing Award.

Also a translator, Crow has published an anthology entitled *Woman Who Has Sprouted Wings: Poems by Contemporary Latin American Women Poets* (Latin American Review Press, 1984; revised edition, 1987), which received a Translation Award from Columbia University's Translation Center. In 1990 Wesleyan University Press will publish *From the Country of Nevermore,* her translations of poems by Jorge Teillier of Chile. In 1982 she traveled in Peru and Chile translating Surrealist poetry on a Fulbright Research Grant.

Mary Crow currently teaches creative writing at Colorado State University in Fort Collins, where she also resides.

BOA EDITIONS, LTD.
NEW POETS OF AMERICA SERIES